THIS BOOK BELONGS TO:

_____

_____

A Simple Guide To Holy Quran Journaling - Devotional & Guided
Prompts With Du'a and Practical Applications.
A Muslim Journal For Spiritual Growth and Development.

Print ISBN-13 : 979-8648933910

For any further inquiries please do not hesitate to contact us at: notespess@mail.com

بِسْمِ اللهِ الرَّحْمٰنِ الرَّحِيْمِ

"فَإِنَّ مَعَ ٱلْعُسْرِ يُسْرًا"

"Indeed With Hardship Comes Ease"

[Quran 94:6]

>What is The Quran?

The Quran is the literal, spoken Word of Allah revealed to the last Prophet Muhammad (AS), may the mercy and blessings of Allah be upon him, through Gabriel, the Angel of Revelation, transmitted to us by numerous channels, both verbally and in written form. Inimitable and unique, it is divinely protected from corruption.

Arabic terms meanings:

>Surah : Chapter of the Quran.

>Juz' : One of thirty parts of the Quran.

>Aayaat : (singular – ayah) the word "aayaat" can have many meanings. It is almost always used when talking about proofs from almighty God Allah. These include verses, lessons, signs, and revelations.

>Du'a : Prayer and supplication.

>Tafsir : Means to explain, to expound, to elaborate or to interpret. The word tafsir is the verbal noun of "fassara" and tafsir means the explanation or interpretation of something.

>Muharram : Muharram is the first month of the Islamic calendar.

>Allahu Akbar : Arabic for "Allah is most great," or "God is great."

This Simple Quran study journal is the perfect companion for you in your Holy Quran journaling & readings and to create a relationship with the words of Allah in your daily life. Whether you're a beginner or someone who used to Quran studying this book is perfect for you to cultivate your relationship with God as you study the Word.

Feel free to use this journal as you want to, each page includes a section for:

>Surah : Start by writing the Surah name.

>Verse : Verse (ayah) number.

>Arabic : Copy the verse in Arabic, it helps you with language practice.

>Translation : Write down the translation that's clear and you best understand.

>Tafsir : Find a good, reliable Tafseer. The Tafseer helps because it gives you much-needed background and context to properly understand what the verses of the Quran mean.

>Notes & Reflection : Write down important aspects of the story that stand out to you and your own thoughts and reflections on the verse. How does this verse connect to you and your experiences? etc... You can simply start off the process with, "this verse reminds me of when..." or "this verse makes me think of....".

>Dua & Practical Applications : Feel free to write a short Du'a and give thanks to the lord beside practical applications that will encourage you to reflect applying God's Word to your own life and heart.

Note : You're not limited to only study one Verse (ayah) per page, You're free to study 1-2 or more Ayaat or a whole Jus' as you prefer.

May Allah accept all your efforts in better connecting with the Quran. Ameen.

Qur'an Structure

Surah Order

Surah	Name	Ayah	Revealed No.	Revealed	Surah	Name	Ayah	Revealed No.	Revealed
	⬇	⬇	⬇	⬇	29	Al-Ankabut	69	85	Mecca 85
1	Al-Fathiha	7	5	Mecca 5	30	Ar-Rum	60	84	Mecca 84
2	Al-Baqara	286	87	Madina 87	31	Luqman	34	57	Mecca 57
3	Al-i'Imran	200	89	Madina 89	32	As-Sajda	30	75	Mecca 75
4	An-Nisaa	176	92	Madina 92	33	Al-Ahzab	73	90	Madina 90
5	Al-Maida	120	112	Madina 112	34	Saba	54	58	Mecca 58
6	Al-An'am	165	55	Mecca 55	35	Fatir	45	43	Mecca 43
7	Al-A'raf	206	39	Mecca 39	36	Ya-Sin	83	41	Mecca 41
8	Al-Anfal	75	88	Madina 88	37	As-Saffat	182	56	Mecca 56
9	At-Tauba	129	113	Madina 113	38	Sad	88	38	Mecca 38
10	Yunus	109	51	Mecca 51	39	Az-Zumar	75	59	Mecca 59
11	Hud	123	52	Mecca 52	40	Al-Mu'min	85	60	Mecca 60
12	Yusuf	111	53	Mecca 53	41	Ha-Mim	54	61	Mecca 61
13	Ar-Ra'd	43	96	Madina 96	42	Ash-Shura	53	62	Mecca 62
14	Ibrahim	52	72	Mecca 72	43	Az-Zukhruf	89	63	Mecca 63
15	Al-Hijr	99	54	Mecca 54	44	Ad-Dukhan	59	64	Mecca 64
16	An-Nahl	128	70	Mecca 70	45	Al-Jathiya	37	65	Mecca 65
17	Al-Israa	111	50	Mecca 50	46	Al-Ahqaf	35	66	Mecca 66
18	Al-Kahf	110	69	Mecca 69	47	Muhammad	38	95	Madina 95
19	Maryam	98	44	Mecca 44	48	Al-Fat-h	29	111	Madina 111
20	Ta-ha	135	45	Mecca 45	49	Al-Hujurat	18	106	Madina 106
21	Al-Anbiyaa	112	73	Mecca 73	50	Qaf	45	34	Mecca 34
22	Al-Hajj	78	103	Madina 103	51	Az-Zariyat	60	67	Mecca 67
23	Al-Muminun	118	74	Mecca 74	52	At-Tur	49	76	Mecca 76
24	An-Nur	64	102	Madina 102	53	An-Najm	62	23	Mecca 23
25	Al-Furqan	77	42	Mecca 42	54	Al-Qamar	55	37	Mecca 37
26	Ash-Shu'araa	227	47	Mecca 47	55	Ar-Rahman	78	97	Madina 97
27	An-Naml	93	48	Mecca 48	56	Al-Waqi'a	96	46	Mecca 46
28	Al-Qasas	88	49	Mecca 49	57	Al-Hadid	29	94	Madina 94

Qur'an Structure

Surah Order

Surah	Name	Ayah	Revealed	No.	Revealed
58	Al-Mujadila	22	105		Madina 105
59	Al-Hashr	24	101		Madina 101
60	Al-Mumtahana	13	91		Madina 91
61	As-Saff	14	109		Madina 109
62	Al-Jamu'a	11	110		Madina 110
63	Al-Munafiqun	11	104		Madina 104
64	At-Tagabun	18	108		Madina 108
65	At-Talaq	12	99		Madina 99
66	At-Tahrim	12	107		Madina 107
67	Al-Mulk	30	77		Mecca 77
68	Al-Qalam	52	2		Mecca 2
69	Al-Haqqa	52	78		Mecca 78
70	Al-Ma'arij	44	79		Mecca 79
71	Nuh	28	71		Mecca 71
72	Al-Jinn	28	40		Mecca 40
73	Al-Muzzammil	20	3		Mecca 3
74	Al-Muddaththir	56	4		Mecca 4
75	Al-Qiyamat	40	31		Mecca 31
76	Ad-Dahr	31	98		Madina 98
77	Al-Mursalat	50	33		Mecca 33
78	An-Nabaa	40	80		Mecca 80
79	An-Nazi'at	46	81		Mecca 81
80	Abasa	42	24		Mecca 24
81	At-Takwir	29	7		Mecca 7
82	Al-Infitar	19	82		Mecca 82
83	Al-Mutaffifin	36	86		Mecca 86
84	Al-Inshiqaq	25	83		Mecca 83
85	Al-Buruj	22	27		Mecca 27
86	At-Tariq	17	36		Mecca 36
87	Al-A'la	19	8		Mecca 8
88	Al-Gashiya	26	68		Mecca 68
89	Al-Fajr	30	10		Mecca 10
90	Al-Balad	20	35		Mecca 35
91	Ash-Shams	15	26		Mecca 26
92	Al-Lail	21	9		Mecca 9
93	Adh-Dhuha	11	11		Mecca 11
94	Al-Sharh	8	12		Mecca 12
95	At-Tin	8	28		Mecca 28
96	Al-Alaq	19	1		Mecca 1
97	Al-Qadr	5	25		Mecca 25
98	Al-Baiyina	8	100		Madina 100
99	Al-Zalzalah	8	93		Madina 93
100	Al-Adiyat	11	14		Mecca 14
101	Al-Qari'a	11	30		Mecca 30
102	At-Takathur	8	16		Mecca 16
103	Al-Asr	3	13		Mecca 13
104	Al-Humaza	9	32		Mecca 32
105	Al-Fil	5	19		Mecca 19
106	Quraish	4	29		Mecca 29
107	Al-Ma'un	7	17		Mecca 17
108	Al-Kauthar	3	15		Mecca 15
109	Al-Kafirun	6	18		Mecca 18
110	An-Nasr	3	114		Madina 114
111	Al-Lahab	5	6		Mecca 6
112	Al-Ikhlaas	4	22		Mecca 22
113	Al-Falaq	5	20		Mecca 20
114	An-Nas	6	21		Mecca 21

Qur'an Structure

Juz	Starting Surah	Ayah
1	1 - Al-Fathiha	1
2	2 - Al-Baqara	142
3	2 - Al-Baqara	253
4	3 - Al-i'Imran	92
5	4 - An-Nisaa	24
6	4 - An-Nisaa	148
7	5 - Al-Maida	83
8	6 - Al-An'am	111
9	7 - Al-A'raf	88
10	8 - Al-Anfal	41
11	9 - At-Tauba	94
12	11 - Hud	6
13	12 - Yusuf	53
14	15 - Al-Hijr	2
15	17 - Al-Israa	1
16	18 - Al-Kahf	75
17	21 - Al-Anbiyaa	1
18	23 - Al-Muminun	1
19	25 - Al-Furqan	21
20	27 - An-Naml	60
21	29 - Al-Ankabut	45
22	33 - Al-Ahzab	31
23	36 - Ya-Sin	22
24	39 - Az-Zumar	32
25	41 - Ha-Mim	47
26	46 - Al-Ahqaf	2
27	51 - Az-Zariyat	31
28	58 - Al-Mujadila	1
29	67 - Al-Mulk	1
30	78 - An-Nabaa	2

Additional pages include a section for:

> What I Learned :
(Write down what you have learned from past verses)
> Lessons That I Cherish
> My Favorite Verses :
(Verses that you loved / The ones that got your attention most)
> Rules To Live By :
(Rules you want to apply in your life)
> Gratitude :
"If You Are Grateful, I Will Surely Increase You [in favor]" [Quran 14:7]
(Express your gratitude (Shukr) Appreciate what you have, many don't have it. Write down the things you're Grateful for.)
> Notes :
(This is your creative space you can scribble, draw, make a checklist, or write down anything you want.)

وَلَقَدْ يَسَّرْنَا الْقُرْآنَ لِلذِّكْرِ فَهَلْ مِن مُّدَّكِرٍ

"And We Have Certainly Made The

Qur'an

Easy For Remembrance So Is
There Any Who Will Remember?"

[Surah Qamar v.17]

Surah: **Verse (ayah):**

Arabic:

Translation:

Tafsir:

Notes & Reflection:

Dua & Practical Applications:

Surah: **Verse (ayah):**

Arabic:

Translation:

Tafsir:

_____
_____
_____
_____

Notes & Reflection:

_____
_____
_____
_____
_____
_____

Dua & Practical Applications:

_____
_____
_____
_____

Surah: **Verse (ayah):**

Arabic:

Translation:

Tafsir:

Notes & Reflection:

Dua & Practical Applications:

What I Learned

_____

_____

_____

_____

Lessons That I Cherish _____

My Favorite Verses:

_____

_____

_____

_____

Rules To Live By:

① _____

② _____

③ _____

④ _____

Gratitude

_____

_____

_____

_____

_____

Surah: **Verse (ayah):**

Arabic: **Translation:**

Tafsir:

Notes & Reflection:

Dua & Practical Applications:

Surah: _____ Verse (ayah): _____

Arabic: _____

Translation:

Tafsir:

_____
_____
_____
_____
_____

Notes & Reflection:

_____
_____
_____
_____
_____
_____
_____

Dua & Practical Applications:

_____
_____
_____
_____

Surah: **Verse (ayah):**

Arabic:

Translation:

Tafsir:

Notes & Reflection:

Dua & Practical Applications:

What I Learned _____

_____

_____

_____

_____

_ Lessons That I Cherish _____

My Favorite Verses:

_____

_____

_____

_____

Rules To Live By:

① _____

② _____

③ _____

④ _____

Notes _____

Surah: **Verse (ayah):**

Arabic:

Translation:

Tafsir:

Notes & Reflection:

Dua & Practical Applications:

Surah: Verse (ayah):

Arabic: ——————

Translation:

Tafsir:

Notes & Reflection:

Dua & Practical Applications:

Surah: **Verse (ayah):**

Arabic: ——————

Translation:

Tafsir:

Notes & Reflection:

Dua & Practical Applications:

What I Learned

_____

_____

_____

_____

_ *Lessons That I Cherish* _____

My Favorite Verses:

_____

_____

_____

_____

_____

Rules To Live By:

① _____

② _____

③ _____

④ _____

Gratitude

_____

_____

_____

_____

Surah: **Verse (ayah):**

Arabic:

Translation:

Tafsir:

_____
_____
_____
_____
_____

Notes & Reflection:

_____
_____
_____
_____
_____
_____

Dua & Practical Applications:

_____
_____
_____
_____

Surah: **Verse (ayah):**

Arabic: ——————

Translation:

Tafsir:

Notes & Reflection:

Dua & Practical Applications:

Surah: **Verse (ayah):**

Arabic:

Translation:

Tafsir:

_____

_____

_____

_____

Notes & Reflection:

_____

_____

_____

_____

_____

_____

Dua & Practical Applications:

_____

_____

_____

_____

What I Learned _____

_____

_____

_____

_____

Lessons That I Cherish _____

My Favorite Verses:

_____

_____

_____

_____

Rules To Live By:

① _____

② _____

③ _____

④ _____

Notes _____

Surah: **Verse (ayah):**

Arabic:

Translation:

Tafsir:

Notes & Reflection:

Dua & Practical Applications:

> **Surah:** **Verse (ayah):**

Arabic:

Translation:

Tafsir:

Notes & Reflection:

Dua & Practical Applications:

Surah: **Verse (ayah):**

Arabic: **Translation:**

Tafsir:

_____
_____
_____
_____

Notes & Reflection:

_____
_____
_____
_____
_____
_____

Dua & Practical Applications:

_____
_____
_____
_____

What I Learned _____

_____

_____

_____

_____

Lessons That I Cherish _____

My Favorite Verses:

_____

_____

_____

_____

_____

Rules To Live By:

① _____

② _____

③ _____

④ _____

Gratitude

_____

_____

_____

_____

_____

Surah: **Verse (ayah):**

Arabic:

Translation:

Tafsir:

Notes & Reflection:

Dua & Practical Applications:

Surah: **Verse (ayah):**

Arabic:

Translation:

Tafsir:

Notes & Reflection:

Dua & Practical Applications:

Surah: **Verse (ayah):**

Arabic:

Translation:

Tafsir:

Notes & Reflection:

Dua & Practical Applications:

What I Learned _____

_____

_____

_____

_____

Lessons That I Cherish _____

My Favorite Verses:

_____

_____

_____

_____

Rules To Live By:

① _____

② _____

③ _____

④ _____

Notes _____

Surah: **Verse (ayah):**

Arabic:

Translation:

Tafsir:

_____

_____

_____

_____

Notes & Reflection:

_____

_____

_____

_____

_____

_____

Dua & Practical Applications:

_____

_____

_____

_____

Surah: **Verse (ayah):**

Arabic: ——————

Translation:

Tafsir:

_____

_____

_____

_____

Notes & Reflection:

_____

_____

_____

_____

_____

Dua & Practical Applications:

_____

_____

_____

_____

Surah: **Verse (ayah):**

Arabic:

Translation:

Tafsir:

_____

_____

_____

_____

Notes & Reflection:

_____

_____

_____

_____

_____

_____

Dua & Practical Applications:

_____

_____

_____

_____

What I Learned _____

_____

_____

_____

_____

_ *Lessons That I Cherish* _____

My Favorite Verses:

_____

_____

_____

_____

_____

Rules To Live By:

① _____

② _____

③ _____

④ _____

Gratitude

_____

_____

_____

_____

_____

Surah: **Verse (ayah):**

Arabic:

Translation:

Tafsir:

Notes & Reflection:

Dua & Practical Applications:

Surah:

Verse (ayah):

Arabic:

Translation:

Tafsir:

Notes & Reflection:

Dua & Practical Applications:

Surah:　　　　　**Verse (ayah):**

Arabic:

Translation:

Tafsir:

_____
_____
_____
_____

Notes & Reflection:

_____
_____
_____
_____
_____
_____

Dua & Practical Applications:

_____
_____
_____
_____

What I Learned _____

_____

_____

_____

Lessons That I Cherish _____

My Favorite Verses:

_____

_____

_____

_____

Rules To Live By:

① _____

② _____

③ _____

④ _____

Notes _____

Surah: **Verse (ayah):**

Arabic:

Translation:

Tafsir:

_____
_____
_____
_____
_____

Notes & Reflection:

_____
_____
_____
_____
_____
_____

Dua & Practical Applications:

_____
_____
_____
_____

Surah: **Verse (ayah):**

Arabic: ────────────

Translation:

Tafsir:

Notes & Reflection:

Dua & Practical Applications:

Surah: **Verse (ayah):**

Arabic:

Translation:

Tafsir:

_____

_____

_____

_____

Notes & Reflection:

_____

_____

_____

_____

_____

_____

Dua & Practical Applications:

_____

_____

_____

_____

What I Learned _____

_____

_____

_____

_____

Lessons That I Cherish _____

My Favorite Verses:

_____

_____

_____

_____

_____

Rules To Live By:

① _____

② _____

③ _____

④ _____

Gratitude

_____

_____

_____

_____

_____

Surah: **Verse (ayah):**

Arabic: **Translation:**

Tafsir:

_____

_____

_____

_____

Notes & Reflection:

_____

_____

_____

_____

_____

_____

Dua & Practical Applications:

_____

_____

_____

_____

Surah: Verse (ayah):

Arabic:

Translation:

Tafsir:

Notes & Reflection:

Dua & Practical Applications:

Surah: **Verse (ayah):**

Arabic: **Translation:**

Tafsir:

_____

_____

_____

_____

Notes & Reflection:

_____

_____

_____

_____

_____

_____

Dua & Practical Applications:

_____

_____

_____

_____

What I Learned _____

_____

_____

_____

_____

Lessons That I Cherish _____

My Favorite Verses:

_____

_____

_____

_____

_____

Rules To Live By:

① _____

② _____

③ _____

④ _____

Notes _____

فَبِأَيِّ آلَاءِ رَبِّكُمَا تُكَذِّبَانِ

"Then Which Of
The Favors Of Your Lord
Would You Deny."

[Surah Ar-Rahman v.36]

Surah: **Verse (ayah):**

Arabic: **Translation:**

Tafsir:

_____
_____
_____
_____

Notes & Reflection:

_____
_____
_____
_____
_____
_____

Dua & Practical Applications:

_____
_____
_____
_____

> **Surah:** **Verse (ayah):**

Arabic:

Translation:

Tafsir:

Notes & Reflection:

Dua & Practical Applications:

Surah: **Verse (ayah):**

Arabic:

Translation:

Tafsir:

_____
_____
_____
_____

Notes & Reflection:

_____
_____
_____
_____
_____
_____

Dua & Practical Applications:

_____
_____
_____
_____

What I Learned _____

_____

_____

_____

_____

Lessons That I Cherish _____

My Favorite Verses:

_____

_____

_____

_____

_____

Rules To Live By:

① _____

② _____

③ _____

④ _____

Gratitude

_____

_____

_____

_____

Surah: **Verse (ayah):**

Arabic:

Translation:

Tafsir:

Notes & Reflection:

Dua & Practical Applications:

Surah: **Verse (ayah):**

Arabic:

Translation:

Tafsir:

_____
_____
_____
_____

Notes & Reflection:

_____
_____
_____
_____
_____
_____

Dua & Practical Applications:

_____
_____
_____
_____

Surah: **Verse (ayah):**

Arabic:

Translation:

Tafsir:

Notes & Reflection:

Dua & Practical Applications:

What I Learned _____

_____

_____

_____

_____

Lessons That I Cherish _____

My Favorite Verses:

_____

_____

_____

_____

_____

Rules To Live By:

① _____

② _____

③ _____

④ _____

_____

Notes _____

Surah: **Verse (ayah):**

Arabic: **Translation:**

Tafsir:

_____
_____
_____
_____

Notes & Reflection:

_____
_____
_____
_____
_____
_____

Dua & Practical Applications:

_____
_____
_____
_____

Surah: **Verse (ayah):**

Arabic:

Translation:

Tafsir:

_____

_____

_____

_____

Notes & Reflection:

_____

_____

_____

_____

_____

_____

Dua & Practical Applications:

_____

_____

_____

_____

Surah: **Verse (ayah):**

Arabic:

Translation:

Tafsir:

_____
_____
_____
_____
_____

Notes & Reflection:

_____
_____
_____
_____
_____
_____
_____

Dua & Practical Applications:

_____
_____
_____
_____

What I Learned _____

_____

_____

_____

_____

Lessons That I Cherish _____

My Favorite Verses:

_____

_____

_____

_____

_____

Rules To Live By:

① _____

② _____

③ _____

④ _____

Gratitude

_____

_____

_____

_____

_____

Surah: **Verse (ayah):**

Arabic:

Translation:

Tafsir:

_____

_____

_____

_____

Notes & Reflection:

_____

_____

_____

_____

_____

_____

Dua & Practical Applications:

_____

_____

_____

_____

Surah: **Verse (ayah):**

Arabic:

Translation:

Tafsir:

_____
_____
_____
_____

Notes & Reflection:

_____
_____
_____
_____
_____
_____

Dua & Practical Applications:

_____
_____
_____
_____

Surah: **Verse (ayah):**

Arabic:

Translation:

Tafsir:

_____
_____
_____
_____
_____

Notes & Reflection:

_____
_____
_____
_____
_____
_____
_____

Dua & Practical Applications:

_____
_____
_____
_____

What I Learned

Lessons That I Cherish

My Favorite Verses:

Rules To Live By:

①

②

③

④

Notes

Surah: **Verse (ayah):**

Arabic:

Translation:

Tafsir:

_____

_____

_____

_____

Notes & Reflection:

_____

_____

_____

_____

_____

_____

Dua & Practical Applications:

_____

_____

_____

_____

Surah:

Verse (ayah):

Arabic:

Translation:

Tafsir:

_____
_____
_____
_____
_____

Notes & Reflection:

_____
_____
_____
_____
_____
_____

Dua & Practical Applications:

_____
_____
_____
_____

Surah: **Verse (ayah):**

Arabic:

Translation:

Tafsir:

_____

_____

_____

_____

Notes & Reflection:

_____

_____

_____

_____

_____

Dua & Practical Applications:

_____

_____

_____

_____

What I Learned _____

_____

_____

_____

_____

Lessons That I Cherish _____

My Favorite Verses:

_____

_____

_____

_____

_____

Rules To Live By:

① _____

② _____

③ _____

④ _____

Gratitude

_____

_____

_____

_____

Surah: **Verse (ayah):**

Arabic:

Translation:

Tafsir:

Notes & Reflection:

Dua & Practical Applications:

> Surah: _____ Verse (ayah): _____

Arabic: _____

Translation:

Tafsir:

_____

_____

_____

_____

Notes & Reflection:

_____

_____

_____

_____

_____

_____

Dua & Practical Applications:

_____

_____

_____

_____

Surah: **Verse (ayah):**

Arabic:

Translation:

Tafsir:

_____
_____
_____
_____

Notes & Reflection:

_____
_____
_____
_____
_____
_____

Dua & Practical Applications:

_____
_____
_____
_____

What I Learned _____

_____

_____

_____

_____

Lessons That I Cherish _____

My Favorite Verses:

_____

_____

_____

_____

_____

Rules To Live By:

① _____

② _____

③ _____

④ _____

_____

Notes _____

Surah: **Verse (ayah):**

Arabic: **Translation:**

Tafsir:

_____
_____
_____
_____

Notes & Reflection:

_____
_____
_____
_____
_____
_____

Dua & Practical Applications:

_____
_____
_____
_____

Surah: Verse (ayah):

Arabic: Translation:

Tafsir:

_____
_____
_____
_____
_____

Notes & Reflection:

_____
_____
_____
_____
_____
_____
_____

Dua & Practical Applications:

_____
_____
_____
_____

Surah: **Verse (ayah):**

Arabic: **Translation:**

Tafsir:

Notes & Reflection:

Dua & Practical Applications:

What I Learned _____

_____

_____

_____

_____

Lessons That I Cherish _____

_____

My Favorite Verses:

_____

_____

_____

_____

_____

Rules To Live By:

① _____

② _____

③ _____

④ _____

Gratitude ♡

_____

_____

_____

_____

_____

Surah: **Verse (ayah):**

Arabic: **Translation:**

Tafsir:

Notes & Reflection:

Dua & Practical Applications:

Surah: **Verse (ayah):**

Arabic:

Translation:

Tafsir:

Notes & Reflection:

Dua & Practical Applications:

Surah: **Verse (ayah):**

Arabic: **Translation:**

Tafsir:

_____

_____

_____

_____

Notes & Reflection:

_____

_____

_____

_____

_____

_____

Dua & Practical Applications:

_____

_____

_____

_____

What I Learned _____

_____

_____

_____

_____

Lessons That I Cherish _____

My Favorite Verses:

_____

_____

_____

_____

_____

Rules To Live By:

① _____

② _____

③ _____

④ _____

Notes _____

Surah: **Verse (ayah):**

Arabic:

Translation:

Tafsir:

_____
_____
_____
_____

Notes & Reflection:

_____
_____
_____
_____
_____
_____

Dua & Practical Applications:

_____
_____
_____
_____

Surah: **Verse (ayah):**

Arabic: **Translation:**

Tafsir:

_____

_____

_____

_____

_____

Notes & Reflection:

_____

_____

_____

_____

_____

_____

Dua & Practical Applications:

_____

_____

_____

_____

Surah: **Verse (ayah):**

Arabic:

Translation:

Tafsir:

_____

_____

_____

_____

_____

Notes & Reflection:

_____

_____

_____

_____

_____

_____

_____

Dua & Practical Applications:

_____

_____

_____

_____

What I Learned _____

_____

_____

_____

_____

Lessons That I Cherish _____

_____

My Favorite Verses:

_____

_____

_____

_____

_____

Rules To Live By:

① _____

② _____

③ _____

④ _____

_____

Gratitude

_____

_____

_____

_____

_____

Surah: **Verse (ayah):**

Arabic:

Translation:

Tafsir:

_____
_____
_____
_____

Notes & Reflection:

_____
_____
_____
_____
_____
_____

Dua & Practical Applications:

_____
_____
_____
_____

Surah: **Verse (ayah):**

Arabic:

Translation:

Tafsir:

_____
_____
_____
_____
_____

Notes & Reflection:

_____
_____
_____
_____
_____
_____
_____

Dua & Practical Applications:

_____
_____
_____
_____

Surah: **Verse (ayah):**

Arabic:

Translation:

Tafsir:

_____
_____
_____
_____

Notes & Reflection:

_____
_____
_____
_____
_____
_____

Dua & Practical Applications:

_____
_____
_____
_____

What I Learned

_____

_____

_____

_____

Lessons That I Cherish

My Favorite Verses:

_____

_____

_____

_____

Rules To Live By:

① _____

② _____

③ _____

④ _____

Notes

رَبَّنَا آتِنَا مِن لَّدُنكَ رَحْمَةً

وَهَيِّئْ لَنَا مِنْ أَمْرِنَا رَشَدًا

"Our Lord, Grant Us From Yourself Mercy And Prepare For Us From Our Affair Right Guidance."

[Surah Al-Kahf v.10]

Surah: **Verse (ayah):**

Arabic:

Translation:

Tafsir:

_____
_____
_____
_____

Notes & Reflection:

_____
_____
_____
_____
_____

Dua & Practical Applications:

_____
_____
_____
_____

Surah: **Verse (ayah):**

Arabic:

Translation:

Tafsir:

_____
_____
_____
_____
_____

Notes & Reflection:

_____
_____
_____
_____
_____
_____
_____

Dua & Practical Applications:

_____
_____
_____
_____

Surah: **Verse (ayah):**

Arabic:

Translation:

Tafsir:

Notes & Reflection:

Dua & Practical Applications:

What I Learned

Lessons That I Cherish

My Favorite Verses:

Rules To Live By:

①

②

③

④

Gratitude

Surah: **Verse (ayah):**

Arabic:

Translation:

Tafsir:

Notes & Reflection:

Dua & Practical Applications:

Surah: **Verse (ayah):**

Arabic: ————

Translation:

Tafsir:

Notes & Reflection:

Dua & Practical Applications:

Surah: **Verse (ayah):**

Arabic: **Translation:**

Tafsir:

Notes & Reflection:

Dua & Practical Applications:

What I Learned _____

_____

_____

_____

_ *Lessons That I Cherish* _____

My Favorite Verses:

_____

_____

_____

_____

Rules To Live By:

① _____

② _____

③ _____

④ _____

Notes _____

Surah: **Verse (ayah):**

Arabic: **Translation:**

Tafsir:

_____
_____
_____
_____
_____

Notes & Reflection:

_____
_____
_____
_____
_____
_____

Dua & Practical Applications:

_____
_____
_____
_____

Surah: _____ Verse (ayah): _____

Arabic: _____

Translation:

Tafsir:

_____
_____
_____
_____

Notes & Reflection:

_____
_____
_____
_____
_____
_____

Dua & Practical Applications:

_____
_____
_____
_____

Surah: **Verse (ayah):**

Arabic:

Translation:

Tafsir:

Notes & Reflection:

Dua & Practical Applications:

What I Learned

_____

_____

_____

_____

Lessons That I Cherish _____

My Favorite Verses:

_____

_____

_____

_____

_____

Rules To Live By:

① _____

② _____

③ _____

④ _____

Gratitude

_____

_____

_____

_____

_____

Surah: _____ **Verse (ayah):** _____

Arabic:

Translation:

Tafsir:

_____
_____
_____
_____

Notes & Reflection:

_____
_____
_____
_____
_____
_____

Dua & Practical Applications:

_____
_____
_____
_____

Surah: **Verse (ayah):**

Arabic: **Translation:**

Tafsir:

Notes & Reflection:

Dua & Practical Applications:

Surah: **Verse (ayah):**

Arabic:

Translation:

Tafsir:

_____
_____
_____
_____
_____

Notes & Reflection:

_____
_____
_____
_____
_____
_____
_____

Dua & Practical Applications:

_____
_____
_____
_____

What I Learned _____

_____

_____

_____

_____

_ Lessons That I Cherish _____

My Favorite Verses:

_____

_____

_____

_____

Rules To Live By:

① _____

② _____

③ _____

④ _____

Notes _____

Surah: **Verse (ayah):**

Arabic:

Translation:

Tafsir:

Notes & Reflection:

Dua & Practical Applications:

> Surah: _____   Verse (ayah): _____

Arabic: ─────────────────┐   Translation:
                         │   ┌─────────────────────────────────
                         │   │
                         │   │
                         │   │
                         │   │
                         │   │
                         │   │
                         │   │
                         │   │
                         │   │
                         │   │
                         │   │
─────────────────────────┘   └─────────────────────────────────

Tafsir:
_____
_____
_____
_____
_____

Notes & Reflection:
_____
_____
_____
_____
_____
_____

Dua & Practical Applications:
_____
_____
_____
_____

Surah: **Verse (ayah):**

Arabic:

Translation:

Tafsir:

_____
_____
_____
_____
_____

Notes & Reflection:

_____
_____
_____
_____
_____
_____
_____

Dua & Practical Applications:

_____
_____
_____
_____

What I Learned _____

_____

_____

_____

_____

Lessons That I Cherish _____

My Favorite Verses:

_____

_____

_____

_____

Rules To Live By:

① _____

② _____

③ _____

④ _____

Gratitude

_____

_____

_____

_____

_____

Surah: **Verse (ayah):**

Arabic:

Translation:

Tafsir:

_____
_____
_____
_____
_____

Notes & Reflection:

_____
_____
_____
_____
_____
_____

Dua & Practical Applications:

_____
_____
_____
_____

Surah: **Verse (ayah):**

Arabic: ——————

Translation:

Tafsir:

_____
_____
_____
_____
_____

Notes & Reflection:

_____
_____
_____
_____
_____
_____
_____

Dua & Practical Applications:

_____
_____
_____
_____

Surah: **Verse (ayah):**

Arabic: **Translation:**

Tafsir:

_____
_____
_____
_____

Notes & Reflection:

_____
_____
_____
_____
_____
_____

Dua & Practical Applications:

_____
_____
_____
_____

What I Learned _____

_____

_____

_____

_____

Lessons That I Cherish _____

My Favorite Verses:

_____

_____

_____

_____

Rules To Live By:

① _____

② _____

③ _____

④ _____

Notes _____

Surah: **Verse (ayah):**

Arabic:

Translation:

Tafsir:

Notes & Reflection:

Dua & Practical Applications:

Surah: **Verse (ayah):**

Arabic:

Translation:

Tafsir:

_____
_____
_____
_____
_____
_____

Notes & Reflection:

_____
_____
_____
_____
_____
_____
_____

Dua & Practical Applications:

_____
_____
_____
_____

Surah: **Verse (ayah):**

Arabic:

Translation:

Tafsir:

_____
_____
_____
_____

Notes & Reflection:

_____
_____
_____
_____
_____
_____
_____

Dua & Practical Applications:

_____
_____
_____
_____

What I Learned _____

_____

_____

_____

_____

— Lessons That I Cherish _____

My Favorite Verses:

_____

_____

_____

_____

Rules To Live By:

① _____

② _____

③ _____

④ _____

Gratitude

_____

_____

_____

_____

Surah: _____ **Verse (ayah):** _____

Arabic:

Translation:

Tafsir:

_____
_____
_____
_____
_____

Notes & Reflection:

_____
_____
_____
_____
_____
_____

Dua & Practical Applications:

_____
_____
_____
_____

Surah: Verse (ayah):

Arabic: ————

Translation:

Tafsir:

Notes & Reflection:

Dua & Practical Applications:

Surah: **Verse (ayah):**

Arabic:

Translation:

Tafsir:

_____
_____
_____
_____
_____

Notes & Reflection:

_____
_____
_____
_____
_____
_____

Dua & Practical Applications:

_____
_____
_____
_____

What I Learned

Lessons That I Cherish

My Favorite Verses:

Rules To Live By:

①

②

③

④

Notes

Surah: **Verse (ayah):**

Arabic:

Translation:

Tafsir:

Notes & Reflection:

Dua & Practical Applications:

Surah:　　　　　　　**Verse (ayah):**

Arabic:

Translation:

Tafsir:

Notes & Reflection:

Dua & Practical Applications:

Surah: **Verse (ayah):**

Arabic:

Translation:

Tafsir:

Notes & Reflection:

Dua & Practical Applications:

What I Learned _____

_____

_____

_____

_____

Lessons That I Cherish _____

_____

My Favorite Verses:

_____

_____

_____

_____

_____

Rules To Live By:

① _____

② _____

③ _____

④ _____

Gratitude _____

_____

_____

_____

_____

Surah: **Verse (ayah):**

Arabic:

Translation:

Tafsir:

_____
_____
_____
_____
_____

Notes & Reflection:

_____
_____
_____
_____
_____
_____

Dua & Practical Applications:

_____
_____
_____
_____

Surah: Verse (ayah):

Arabic: —————

Translation:

Tafsir:

_____
_____
_____
_____
_____

Notes & Reflection:

_____
_____
_____
_____
_____
_____
_____

Dua & Practical Applications:

_____
_____
_____
_____

Surah: **Verse (ayah):**

Arabic:

Translation:

Tafsir:

_____
_____
_____
_____

Notes & Reflection:

_____
_____
_____
_____
_____
_____

Dua & Practical Applications:

_____
_____
_____
_____

What I Learned _____

_____

_____

_____

_____

Lessons That I Cherish _____

My Favorite Verses:

_____

_____

_____

_____

Rules To Live By:

① _____

② _____

③ _____

④ _____

Notes _____

Reading Log

Day	Juz/Surah	Verse	To Verse

"Read! In The Name Of Your Lord, Who Has Created" [Quran 96:1]

Day	Juz/Surah	Verse	To Verse

Additional Resources:

You can use these websites to help you out with your journey to build a better relationship with the Quran.

https://legacy.quran.com
- (Quran With The Translation)

https://recitequran.com
- (Recites The Word You Click On Along With The Display Of Its Meaning)

https://learningquranonline.com/download-quran/download-tafseer
- (You Can Download Tafseer or Read It Online)

https://www.islamicstudies.info/tafheem.php
- (Another Beautiful Tafseer You Can Choose Any Surah You Want)

https://aimanquranacademy.com
- (An Online Quran Academy)

This book is also available in a 300-page format paperback & hardback ASIN: B08PIFC4Z7
Thank you for purchasing this journal we hope it meet your expectation, get the most out of it, and benefit from it both in belief and action, also in any other criteria of your life. !

NOTES
PRESS

Creating books with a purpose.

Printed in Great Britain
by Amazon

39718704R00077